The Key to Character

THE KEY TO CHARACTER

The Key to Character

THE KEY TO CHARACTER

BY

KHALID EL BEY

DEYEL PUBLISHING COMPANY
SYRACUSE, NEW YORK

CREATIVE RESEARCH SOCIETY
SYRACUSE, NEW YORK

The Key to Character

ISBN: 9780615237435

The Key To Character. Copyright © September 14, 2007 Published by Deyel Publishing, Syracuse, New York.

All Rights Reserved. No part of this book may be used in any manner whatsoever without written permission from the publisher, except in the case of brief quotations embodied in critical articles and reviews.

Printed 2007 and 2010

Cover illustration by Khalid El Bey

Published by
DEYEL PUBLISHING
Syracuse, New York

CREATIVE RESEARCH SOCIETY
Syracuse New York

Printed in the United States of America.

ACKNOWLEDGEMENTS

The Author wishes to thank the following individuals who contributed to the manifestation of this book:

Professor Howard Gordon at Oswego State University for sharing his expertise in the proper use of the English language.

Carolyn Haughton for providing her thoughts on The Key to Character in its forward.

Dr. Donald C. Sawyer III, who took time while working on his Ph.D. to write the Introduction of this book.

The Key to Character

DEDICATION

To those who work in the struggle, not because it is easy, but because it is necessary: Schym Bey, Aziza Clunie, Eric Glover, Taran Aseela Ali, Divad Sanders, Neshecle Senior, and Omar Senior. Your contribution is noted and it matters.

To my stars: Jarez Slater-Bey, Nadia Amani Bey, Saif Ahad El Bey, and Naila Bey. Everything written here was written with you in mind. Make sure you read it.

And to the many not named here who carry the work forward in ways both seen and unseen, this is for you as well.

CONTENTS

Chapter

Forward	*8*
Introduction	*10*
1. My Mind or Yours	15
2. Living the Lie	23
3. Fear	29
4. Selfishness	36
5. Responsibility	47
6. The Key: Discipline	56
7. Who Am I	65
About the Author	67

FORWARD

The Key to Character

The Key to Character is thought provoking. It scrutinizes the psyche, social conditioning theory and alleged politically correct norms. Like being in a courtroom, the arguments presented by the prosecuting attorney and the defense attorney to persuade a jury of one's guilt or innocence, is largely determined by the most convincing presentation of the evidence and facts. The final outcome does not mean that the truth has prevailed or the majority should rule. That said, the Author challenges the assumption of those who suggest one's self worth has much to do with level of education, the three C's (cash, class and color), worldly possessions (a fine home, luxury cars) and personal relationships (the who's who you rub shoulders with). Rather, character is about compassion, sensitivity, integrity, respect for self as well as others and the freedom to explore and test what we instinctively feel is different and unique without ridicule.

- Carolyn Haughton, B.A. Psychology

INTRODUCTION

BECOMING A JEWEL
(Life's perfecting/polishing journey)

The Key to Character

I love Hip-Hop! Though the culture has drifted far off the path of its foundation and most of the original tenets are overshadowed by misogyny and violence, the more positive aspects exude intellectual energy and creativity. Some of the great lyricists (Notorious B.I.G., Jay Z, Kanye West) are able to play with words in ways that academically trained scholars can only dream. With that being said I will do as the aforementioned Emcees by 'playing' with the word "character" in this introduction.

Are we living in a world built on character or a world full of characters? Are we a people of great character or are we characters participating in this world's show? I would argue that we live in a society with an abundance of characters that lack character. What do we do about this? With so many worldly influences and external voices telling us how we should act, who we should date, what clothes we should wear, what kind of car we should drive; it takes a strong, self secured individual to put up and hold in place a force-field to block out these negative stimuli. It takes a great deal of effort to go through the day constantly guarding against all that we encounter that is created to influence and control our choices and decisions. If we let down this protective barrier, we run the risk of becoming mindless drones aimlessly wondering the earth until the day we go to the grave.

If you are reading this now, you have already taken a step towards beginning or continuing your self-initiating process of improving or perfecting your character, which will then have a positive impact on your circles of influence. The perfection of character is no easy task. As mentioned earlier, the societal influential machine is a serious force that is not easily defeated. The perfection of character is a painstaking process of continual self examination filled with mental, emotional and spiritual searching and pruning. Many gardeners will tell you a plant that is pruned has the ability to grow faster and stronger than those allowed to grow unchecked or unguided. The pruning process fosters the removal of distractions, while allowing all positive energies to be transmitted into those areas that are in need of development. The perfecting of character mirrors this pruning process.

As you move along through this process of growing towards self-perfection, keep ever mindful the fact that there will be trials and tribulations. This soul searching may bring a multitude of sensitive areas to the forefront that will need to be dealt with in the appropriate manner. Some of our being has to be fostered and fertilized, while other parts of our self will need to be DESTROYED. A seed dies in the ground before new life can sprout. When you dive into the knowledge that this book provides, be sure to not do so blindly and take every word at face value…that would be religious. Instead, use these words as a catalyst to begin or continue your adventures of self study, correction, and intellectual attainment. I end this introduction with the words of an African proverb, "A jewel is not polished without rubbing; neither is a person without trials." Read this book and search for your personal key.

- Dr. Don C. Sawyer III, Ph. D

Chapter 1

MY MIND OR YOURS
(I live by your standards)

Many times I've had discussions with people, whether it was in an open discussion or forum, or a personal conversation, about the differences between what we believe, what we have been conditioned to think or believe and what it is that we actually know. These discussions have led me to think about how people live out their entire lives according to or circled around some idea that someone else had developed. In our lives, these ideas become the principles, the laws or standards by which we measure ourselves and/or by which we live. This type of conditioning exist within all cultures throughout the world; whether related to religion, economics, fashion or any other ideas or images that might attract our attention during any particular phase in our lives. For the most part anybody would say to you that this is fine, to each's own, whatever works for you; my only concern is, with most of what a lot of us have been conditioned to think, very, very few of us have ever questioned, not the source of the idea(s), but our reason(s) for accepting the idea(s). Take for instance the touchiest subject of all subjects, religion. I have personally talked to numerous people and have asked them why; why do they think or believe as they do in regards to their respective religions? Quite a few of the initial responses were, "because this is what I want or choose to believe"; but as I questioned further the answers would change to, "because this is what my Mother or Father taught me to believe". Ok, I'll accept that, but where did your Mother and / or Father get the idea(s) from and have they ever questioned their reasons for accepting whatever ideas they have accepted about religion? I doubt it. Nine times out of ten, they are only doing as 'they' were told to do.

Now this is not an attack on religion, for there are numerous ideas, fads, etc., they may be considered principles upon which many people base their lives. Let us take a quick look at fashion. The fashion world with all of its glitz and glamour has created a standard, which causes many people around the world to drive themselves insane or into poverty by trying to keep up with the high cost of clothing and jewelry. If you are not wearing certain fashion names or labels; if you're not wearing at least some of the most expensive wears or jewelry; then you are not socially accepted in some circles. Take a look at what the music and television industry has done to young people generation after generation.

How about the type of vehicle you drive or whether you are slim or fat; the type of job you have or whether or not you have some sort of college degree? Hey, popular culture is what it is and we love it. Without a doubt, any type of progress is good and 'is' needed, but what about the damage that is done or the confusion that is created by these things, these ideas?

With a little research, I have found that a good portion of the people who are in need of mental health services or treatment, have acquired their condition due to some kind of substance abuse. I have also found that a lot of these same people, who have used drugs or are using drugs, began using drugs while in junior high or high school. Some of them began using drugs, because they were not accepted in certain social circles or were made to be seen as social outcast, due to their look, style of dress, nationality, etc. Others began using drugs, because they somehow developed the idea that this was the socially acceptable thing to do.

People argue and fight on behalf of religion, music, style of dress, ideas of love or what is morally correct or incorrect. I have sarcastically said to many people in discussions or debates that "you are speaking to me with somebody else's tongue or thinking with somebody else's brain." I mean, without a doubt a lot of what we learn comes by way of some idea that someone else has had at some time in the past, and it is very practical to say that with thorough research and experimentation a man could adopt an idea or make that idea 'his own' by taking the time to 'know' whether the idea is realistic for him personally or for others universally; but instead of knowing for sure, most of us just tread through life believing what we hear, seldom bothering to check the validity of anything.

The Key to Character

My point is this, a lot of us spend a life time trying our hardest to live up to and satisfy some standard, only to fall into depression, and develop feelings of inadequacy; thinking that we are not good enough, smart enough, cool enough, pretty or slim enough; thinking that we do not have enough money, a nice enough house or car, all because we are unsuccessful in our attempts to achieve some goal set for us by someone else. Let us revisit the subject of belief in religion. Most people who hold on to religious beliefs do so, because of fear. We were told when we were young that if we did not believe in God, Allah, etc. that we would burn for eternity in hell. How scary of an idea is that for a young child? Most people who struggle and stress them selves out to keep up with some standard do so, because of the fear of not being accepted. The many standards set for us by our families, our friends or social circles and society as a whole, have caused a large number of us to think that to not satisfy these standards means that we are failures. It is this fear of failing or the fear of being ridiculed for failing that keeps us chasing the ghost. What a way to live your life.

Chapter 2

LIVING THE LIE
(Personality vs. Character)

"I never wear anything cheap; every article of clothing I buy has to be top of the line. I drive one of the most expensive luxury cars.... you know how it is, I have to maintain my image." This same person who made this statement works at a job that pays him just under $9 per hour; that is approximately $17,000 per year (before taxes). He lives in an apartment, where the rent is 500 dollars a month. When you factor in 100 to 200 dollars monthly for utilities, 100 to 200 dollars monthly for food, don't forget the expensive 250 to 350 dollar a month car note and the 200 to maybe 400 dollar a month shopping habit, you have to wonder if this guy has even a penny left at the end of the month?

How many people do you know who are living far beyond their means? I am sure you know quite a few; this may even be you. How do you feel when you have worked so hard in school to receive your bachelor's degree, you find a decent job, make a decent living, yet you still feel empty, and unsatisfied; you feel that what you have achieved is not enough, so you go back to school and spend more money chasing degree after degree? We spend so much time trying to keep up, that we lose sight of who we truly are and our entire life becomes a very uncomfortable and dissatisfying lie.

Let us take a turn and approach this from a different angle. People like what is satisfying to the senses. Your wife or mother bakes cookies and offers you one. The cookie tastes so good that it causes you to say, 'give me another'. An acquaintance of yours walks by and rubs your shoulders and it felt good, so you say to him or her, "hey, do that again". The opposite of that of course is true if the cookie tastes awful or if the acquaintance hurts you when he or she rubs your shoulders. People like what feels (or tastes) good to the senses, so what feels good to us we like; whatever it is that we like we take an interest in (this is signified by the desire to re-live the satisfying sensation); what we take interest in, we're attracted to, whatever attracts us, we pay attention to. Whatever has or controls your attention, controls YOU. Throughout our lives we have numerous experiences, some good and some 'bad'. The things that we like or enjoy, we indulge in. The things that hurt us or that we don't enjoy, we build a sort of protective barrier against them; and so throughout our life experiences, we go through this continual shaping and molding, until we create an idea of or about ourselves that is comforting (to us). This created idea is what we present to the world; this is our personality. The problem with this is that 'who' we are in presentation to the world and who we are when we are all alone is two different people (or many different people, depending on the individual). What you are experiencing, while alone 'in your own counsel' is your true character; that part of you that admits its weaknesses and knows the real reason(s) for all that it does. Now picture this; we go through our daily lives presenting to others what 'we know' is not genuine. How many times have you dreaded the idea of walking into a situation where you knew you would have to laugh at jokes that weren't funny; or keep a smile on your face, and all the while knowing that the people with whom you are dealing are themselves, phony and back stabbing? How uncomfortable is that? I mean, why would you laugh if the joke(s) aren't funny? Why would you put yourself through the turmoil of being around people, who you know are phony or backstabbing? In a world full of illusion it can be very hard for a person to know or recognize truth. It is as if our analytical or reasoning faculties have been purposely 'short-circuited'. So now in this present lifetime, we are faced with what appears to be an impossible task; that of getting re-acquainted with ourselves. All of your life you've assumed that you knew who you were, what your abilities are or what it is that you want out of life; but the fact is you don't know who you are. This is why you cannot make your relationships work or why you cannot find a career that is satisfying. How many people can 'truly' say that they behave in public, as they behave when they are all alone, in their own counsel? Not many. In fact, with the many faces that most of us wear in our attempts to satisfy the many standards that have been set for us by others, who has time to be themselves?

Chapter 3

FEAR

(Of embarrassment)

A lot of times we wonder what it is about people that causes them to posture themselves in a way that suggests that they are without fear or weakness? What is it that causes a person to so aggressively express that which they themselves know to be untrue? Let us revisit an idea that was presented in the previous chapter regarding how personality is developed over a period of time based on our experiences.

When a child is born, he or she is born in virtue; but as a person travels through the maze of standards established by one's peers and society, his / her thinking becomes vague. In the city of Syracuse (New York), there has been an increase in violence; teen violence in particular. Some may attempt to argue that what I am about to say is untrue; my suggestion is that you at least take this into consideration. Think about the message that is communicated through music and / or entertainment, television and movies. It is from these media outlets that standards in fashion, use of language, personal relationships and general behavior are developed in our youth and young adults, in particular. A person who lives in a financially desolate situation and desires to change her condition (based on what she sees on television, what she hears in music or what her friends say "is hot"), but lacks the ability to do so, in an attempt to satisfy the many standards set by peer groups and society, will resort to doing whatever is necessary to satisfy such standards, with hopes of avoiding ridicule if unfortunately, she fails to succeed. So many of these standards are considered unachievable by most people; to avoid embarrassment the individual who is incapable of achieving the standard downplays the standard as unimportant, or worse, overexerts herself in a way that is detrimental not only to herself, but also to others.

Feelings of inadequacy causes a lot of people to feel weak, unfulfilled, and in some ways, targeted. To avoid the embarrassment related to the exposure of weakness, an individual will lie, steal, cheat, and even resort to violence in the name of self-preservation. What causes a man to argue with his mate about a matter in which he knew he was wrong? What causes a person to debate a subject that they know they have never researched or studied? What is it that causes a student to lash out at his teacher, when the teacher is merely asking the student a question relative to his lesson? What is it that causes one person to feel threatened by the mere presence of another person? What is it that causes the divide between the younger people and older people in the community? What is it that creates competition between men in the weight room or women in the beauty parlor? All of these things are created by the idea that one is not reaching a plateau set by someone else.

Consider the high school drop-out rate. The failure of most teenagers to complete high school is more than likely directly related to feelings of pressure stemming from an inability to maintain the status quo in fashion, style, attitude and even test or report card grades. What about the person who acquired the grades necessary for high school graduation, but didn't acquire high enough scores to attend a credible university? There are even some students who consider an education from a community college to be less valuable than an education from a four year school. The idea is that a person who is without an education from a credible four-year school, the chances of succeeding are less than that of a person with a four year degree.

The Key to Character

Imagine what it does to the morale of a person to have feelings of not having done enough. It almost seems as if society is structured in a way that causes people to fail; or at least to cause them to think that they have failed. To live in a society that is built on illusions of value, causes one to chase an idea of success that is ever evasive. It would be easy for one to claim that the society in which we live is one that breeds jealousy, hatred, violence and failure by providing people with tools for building beautiful air castles, but not with the practical sense, skill and ability required to make any of these dreams materialize. What we have instead is a society built on lies, and a people who now unconsciously perpetuate their own destruction; a conglomerate of communities inhabited by a confused people with no real sense of value. What a situation like this creates in those inhabitants is a total disrespect and disregard for others and the community in which they live.

This is not an attempt to put the blame on the society wherein we live; nor is it an attempt to cause the reader to do the same. What it is, is an attempt to empower the reader enough so that he or she may realize that there is no need for fear, and their inability to purchase expensive clothing or attract attention doesn't in any way decrease their value.

Chapter 4

SELFISHNESS

(As long as I look & feel good, who cares if you do?)

I remember there was an incident where a young kid who lived next-door to me was the victim of a shooting. I looked out the door and I could see his mother crying. His other family members were pulling up in their vehicles. What I remember most was a statement made by someone standing close by. A woman standing in her doorway one house away from me said, "I'm glad that wasn't my son." What would cause a person to totally disregard the fact that a young person and his family suffered such a tragedy?

Some of us have seen this type of scenario on more than one occasion. Some of us have even been that person — like the woman one house away from me. Most people are too caught up in their own trials and tribulations to be concerned about another person's problems. As long as we're not having any hard times, who cares if anybody else is.

But here is the question worth sitting with: can this disregard for your fellow man be traced back to those same feelings of inadequacy described in the previous chapters? I would argue that it can — and that it must be, if we are going to be honest about what selfishness actually is and where it actually comes from.

Selfishness is not simply greed. It is not merely the desire to have more than your share. At its root, selfishness is a survival response — the behavior of a person who, somewhere beneath the surface of their daily life, does not believe there is enough: enough safety, enough significance, enough value to go around. A person who is secure in their own worth does not need to diminish another to feel elevated. A person who genuinely believes in their own value does not need to take from someone else to feel whole. It is the person who has been conditioned to chase an external standard they can never fully reach — the person described in every chapter preceding this one — who becomes capable of sacrificing another human being for the sake of their own relief.

Selfishness, in other words, is inadequacy in action.

Once that is understood, the behavior stops being mysterious. It becomes predictable. And what is predictable can be recognized — and eventually corrected.

Let us look at the evidence.

A man and a woman had been dating for a couple of years. During the course of their relationship the woman made complaints that the man hadn't been paying enough attention to her. One day the man decides to end what he considered to be a trying relationship. A couple of weeks later, while walking down the street, the man sees his ex-girlfriend with a new male friend. Naturally this sighting evoked some former feelings. Later that evening the man decides to call his ex-girlfriend to tell her that he misses her and that he wants her back.

Here is the reality: the man does not want the woman back because he misses her. What is true is that he does not want to see any other man with her. His motives are selfish. But look deeper. What is actually driving that selfishness? The sight of another man with his ex-girlfriend activated something — the familiar fear of inadequacy, the fear of not being enough, the fear that someone else is more valuable than he is. His reaching back for her is not love. It is the desperate act of a person trying to quiet the voice of inadequacy by reclaiming what he had discarded. He is not thinking about her feelings. He cannot afford to. He is too busy managing his own pain. This is inadequacy in action — dressed up as longing.

Consider another scenario. In a high school setting we have two young ladies — one who is popular and desires more popularity, and one who is not so popular. Whenever the unpopular girl passes through the hallway the popular girl makes it her business to make fun of her, to generate laughs from her peers. Ask yourself: what is this popular girl actually doing? She is purchasing her own sense of adequacy at the expense of another person's dignity. Every laugh she generates at the unpopular girl's expense is a temporary relief from her own fear of not being enough. The cruelty is not the point. The relief is the point. The cruelty is simply the cost she is willing to make someone else pay for it.

The same mechanism — inadequacy seeking relief at another's expense — operates identically at every level of human society. The person who sabotages a colleague's career to secure their own position.

The drug dealer who sells to a mother of small children, telling himself that her choices are not his responsibility. The person who gossips and destroys a reputation to elevate their own standing in a room. The man who raises his hand against a woman to silence the weakness he cannot bear to face in himself. The woman who takes out her frustrations on her child because she has no other place to put the weight of her own failures. Each of these is the same act — the act of a person who has been so thoroughly conditioned to chase an unattainable standard that they have lost the capacity to absorb their own pain without transferring it to someone else.

And it does not stop at the personal level. Scale the same inadequacy up through the layers of power and the behavior is identical. The politician who sends young men and women to die in a war that serves his financial interests is not categorically different from the popular girl in the hallway. He is purchasing his own relief — his own sense of power, significance, and control — at someone else's ultimate expense. The pharmaceutical company that creates a drug for an ailment, knowing it will produce another ailment that will require another drug, is not operating from a different principle than the drug dealer on the corner. The mechanism is the same. Only the suit is different.

Most people will never connect these behaviors to the unreachable standards established by society and relentlessly promoted by the media, by our peers, and by our families. But each of us is a product of this conditioning. Even I have to remind myself from time to time that the illusions of value promoted in this society are not valuable at all. The tragedy is not simply that people pursue these illusions. The tragedy is that in pursuing them, they lose the capacity for genuine consideration of the people around them — and the community, the family, the nation, is slowly hollowed out from the inside.

When the standard cannot be reached — and by design, it rarely can be — what fills the space where dignity should be is a quiet desperation. And quiet desperation, when it has no honest outlet, becomes selfishness. It becomes the woman in the doorway who cannot feel the grief of her neighbor, because she is too busy being relieved that the grief is not hers. It becomes the man on the phone asking for a woman back, not because he loves her, but because loving himself has become too difficult.

The antidote is not simply telling people to be less selfish. People do not become selfish because no one told them not to be. They become selfish because no one helped them find the thing inside themselves that is genuinely valuable — the thing that exists before the job title, before the reputation, before the possessions, before the performance. Until a person finds that, they will continue to need something from the outside to feel whole. And a person who needs something from the outside to feel whole will always, eventually, take it from someone else.

This is the cost of the lie. And we are all paying it.

Chapter 5

RESPONSIBILITY

The Key to Character

(For your thoughts and actions)

What has become funny to me over time is a statement made by people who may have been found guilty of even the smallest thing: "the Devil made me do it". Most of what happens to people is always somebody else's fault. Very seldom do you hear a man claim responsibility for his misfortune. As stated in a previous chapter, it is not the intent of the author to blame society for any individual's lack of achievement. While the cause of the problem may be social engineering, our knowledge of the existence of this social engineering empowers us with the ability to bring an end to this mental and emotional enslavement.

Every man or woman, who is guilty of damaging his or her personal relationship, blames the other person for their relationship's failure. Every drug dealer or burglar who gets caught, blames society and asserts that a lack of job opportunity is the cause of his trying to "eat fast for free". Every pedophile or child molester blames his or her family and a bad early childhood for an inability to control their hormones or to get a date with someone their own age. Every person found guilty of gang activity, blames the other members of the other gangs for their involvement in questionable activity. Nobody wants to take responsibility for their own actions!

A woman is walking home from work. Every day it takes the woman 30 minutes to get from her job to her house. On her way home, she passes an alleyway and she thinks, "if I take the alley I would get home 15 minutes faster than I would if I walked my normal route." Then she also thinks, "but if I take the alleyway, something could happen to me". So every day this woman walked home from work passing the alleyway and ignoring the temptation to take the shorter and faster route for fear that danger lurked there. One day she leaves work feeling a little more fatigued than usual. She approaches the alleyway and decides that today she's going to take the faster route. She walks through the alleyway and as she gets halfway through the alley, a strange man jumps out from behind a garbage dumpster and rapes her. Here's the question: which person initially had the most control over the potential outcome of this situation? Even though the man should probably be castrated for the crime he committed, the choice to either take the longer or shorter route was ultimately hers. Intuition told her that there would be danger in the alley; nevertheless, for the sake of convenience, she chose to ignore her good conscience and go the shorter, more dangerous route.

The Key to Character

How many times have you heard a person say, "even though the relationship was bad and she cheated on me most of the time, 50% of the responsibility was mine, because I chose to be in that relationship?" Nothing happens to any person without that person first exercising the right to choose. Is this point not true even for the unlucky soul, who attends a nightclub and after the club closes he walks outside and becomes an innocent victim of a drive-by shooting? "The bullet wasn't intended for him" is what people would say, but the fact is that the bullet was intended for him. Prior to leaving for the club, this young man contemplated whether he should go out or stay home. The feeling that he shouldn't go was probably stronger than his desire to be there yet, as time progressed, his desire to go to the club increased and eventually overpowered his good conscience and so fate awaited him.

Some may consider these examples extreme, but in some of our lives these examples all too familiar. The power to choose is the personal property of every single person living on this planet. No one has the right or ability to interfere when an individual is deciding a course of action. Except in the case of small children, who in many cases act or behave in accordance to their parent's will.

Let us consider a woman who is a single parent raising three kids on her own. She has an okay job, but it doesn't pay enough for her to cover the cost of her bills and still have money left over for recreation. Knowing that her electricity bill is due, she gambles and decides to splurge a little at the mall, thinking that she will find the money from some other source to cover her bill. Soon the bill is past due and she doesn't have the money. At this point, she begins to worry and stress, and the effects of how she is thinking and feeling is felt by everyone in the house. If she had only made the right choice and paid her bill, she would not have been in such a tight situation. As in the aforementioned scenarios, the choice and therefore, the outcome of the situation was totally in her control and consequently her responsibility.

In principle the idea that every man or woman is responsible for the choices that he or she makes is true for everyone. There is no part of our day, where we are not faced with the responsibility of making a choice. Our power to choose allows us the opportunity to shape our circumstances, which means that our lives move according to our dictation. Even in religion, people would rather give credit to someone or something that they have never seen, even though they have actively (consciously) carried out a deed without noticeable assistance. There is very, very little that happens to anyone that is not the responsibility of the person(s) in question. Everything that transpires in our lives is the direct result of our thoughts and actions. We are the architects or designers of our own fate, the outcome of which is of our doing and our doing alone. No one can ever be the blame for anything that has ever happened in my life; certainly not in my adult life. Every broken bone, every bad relationship, any financial troubles, any conflict of any sort, and any other thing that has happened or will happen to me, good or bad, has happened or will happen as a result of the choices that I have made or will make. While we may not control the cause of every situation, by choosing how or finding better ways to handle adversity we can indeed be instrumental in determining the outcome(s).

Chapter 6

THE KEY: DISCIPLINE

(Avoid repeating experiences)

There is nothing worse than reliving the same horrible experiences over and over again, but for most people this is a common occurrence. Whether we are talking about dead-end jobs, financial struggles, trying relationships, unworthy friendships, or trouble with the law, many people struggle with the problem of reliving undesirable situations. As with any endeavor, to assure success, some sort of strategic or structured plan is required. In order for children to learn, a curriculum must be structured. In order for a business of any kind to succeed a structured format for how a product should be made or sold is needed. Even nature provides its structure for all that lives or moves within it. Structure trains a person to move with precision and such requires discipline. What is it that causes a person to re-do that which is undesirable? It makes me think back to the movie "Groundhog Day" with Bill Murray, where every morning when he woke up, he would repeat the same day, seeing the same faces, until he decided one day that each day he would try something different. The same holds true for the many people in this world who experience Groundhog Day. The clinical definition for insanity is defined by a person doing the same thing over and over again and each time expecting a different result. A man who has run headfirst into a brick wall would be a fool to get up and run headfirst into that brick wall again. What is wrong with the thinking of a woman who leaves one abusive relationship only to walk straight into another one? What is wrong with the repeat felon, knowing that selling narcotics or robbing banks landed him in jail the first time, but who goes right back into the street and attempts to do it again, somehow thinking that this time he will get away? What is wrong with the thinking of the teenager who is picked on every day by his "friends", yet when tomorrow arrives, he goes right back to that same group of unworthy friends? What is wrong with the person who continually blows money time and time again, all the while knowing that there are bills that have to be paid; and when the bill is past due, he will relive the same stressful moment, month after month after month? As mentioned in earlier chapters, throughout our lives we encounter numerous experiences, each of which is to prepare us for the next experience. Each personal relationship is merely a lesson to prepare us for the <u>one</u> relationship that we could potentially succeed in. The idea is that we learn from the mistakes that we have made in previous situations, so as to avoid repeating the same mistakes in our next or future situation(s). If there are certain characteristics that a woman recognizes in a new or potential mate, which she saw in a mate who abused her in a previous relationship, that woman should have the good sense to walk away from that new person and never look back. Once a person who has served time in jail for committing a crime is released, he, based on past experience(s) should know that he probably needs to try something different. The high school student who feels embarrassed, because he or she has to repeat the same grade should learn from his or her discomfort and make better decisions the second time around, so not to relive the same type of embarrassment again. The unfortunate reality is that most people never learn from their mistakes and so, their lives are a repeat of the same hell over and over again. The key to avoiding these uncomfortable situations is discipline. A man breaks the heart of a woman by ending their relationship. As the woman reflects, she realizes that the relationship wasn't that good for her anyway. One month later, the guy comes back and says to the woman, we should give it another try. The first thought that enters the woman's head is a resounding "NO!"; but as the man continues to talk, the woman begins to reflect on the good times, her emotions begin to build, and she says, "Okay, we can give it another try". Many of us have been in this situation before, so we know the outcome. More than likely the relationship ended again, and for the same reason(s) that it ended before. The mistake made by the woman was ignoring the first response she had in good conscience. If she had only exercised a little discipline and went with her first response she would've never relived such an uncomfortable and unfulfilling situation.

Discipline is the key to a person regaining their personal freedom. There is no other principle more important in this lifetime, for it takes discipline to succeed at anything. To be loyal in a relationship requires discipline. To be prompt for and to be effective in an occupation requires discipline. To be fair and just in all of your dealings, even when others aren't requires discipline. To take a back seat to someone who may be more talented than you, without developing feelings of envy, requires discipline. To draw a straight line requires discipline. To control your emotions or anger in the face of adversity requires discipline. To be courteous to others requires discipline. To appreciate and allow evolution to take place in any respect requires discipline. There is nothing in life that escapes the need for structure / discipline. To be in public, as you are when you are all alone requires discipline. The problem with this idea is that to be disciplined requires too much responsibility for the average person. They would much rather, as mentioned in a previous chapter, pawn the responsibility for their life onto someone else.

No man or woman will ever reclaim his or her life, reshape his or her circumstances, improve his or her personal relationships or friendships, changed their financial conditions, maintain good mental and physical health, or find happiness without first acquiring the required discipline needed to achieve any of the above or any of the many things not mentioned here. It is time that we as individuals stand up and take responsibility for ourselves and our direction... Discipline is the key.

Chapter 7

WHO AM I
(What is my real value?)

Who am I? This is the question of a lifetime, for if we all knew the answer none of us would have any trouble facing our problems. I have asked many people over the years the question "who are you?" What is interesting is that almost none of the people of whom I've asked this question had an answer. How is that? Most of the time when this question is asked the person responding answers by explaining "what they are" and not "who they are." With trying to satisfy so many standards established by or within society, it is very easy for a person to lose sight of who they really are. Most people identify themselves with the occupation they have or by the things they possess. Instead of finding that thing about themselves that makes them genuinely valuable, they validate themselves by what they own or by the people with whom they associate. A person who is known for his great ability in the game of basketball floats into oblivion once his basketball career is over, because as far as he knows, this was the one thing of value that he possessed. This assumed value he received via the standards established within society. Unfortunately for him, once his value has diminished in the eyes of society, it has simultaneously diminished within him. Absent basketball, who would've ever known him anyway?

There are many people who seek this type of validation from sources outside of themselves. If you are good at basketball, or if you desire to be good at basketball, do it because you love the game — not because of the status and reputation you think you will acquire as a result. To practice and improve your skill for the purpose of notoriety will only prove disappointing in the end. Most people who play basketball will never reach the collegiate or professional level, but the person who loves the game will continue to play regardless of the recognition he or she receives.

In principle, the same applies to any person in any profession. A lawyer loses his job and his world crumbles. A man is rejected by his friends and his sense of personal value disappears. A woman who was once poor marries a wealthy man. One day the man files for divorce and because of the prenuptial agreement the woman leaves in the same condition she arrived in: poor. This is a tragic situation, because not only did she not use the time to invest in herself, but most of her time was spent telling her family and friends how she didn't have to work and how her man took care of her. She validated herself by his occupation and his successes, none of which she could take credit for. This is the end of the world for her, because he was her savior — and now she is right back in the situation she dreads the most.

Sit back and think for a moment: who would you be absent your occupation, your personal possessions, or your social affiliations? You wouldn't be the basketball player. You wouldn't be the lawyer. You wouldn't be the politician. You wouldn't be the notorious drug dealer. You wouldn't be the class bully. You wouldn't be the movie star, the singer, the professor, the judge, the Executive Director. You wouldn't be the firefighter or the police officer. You wouldn't be the factory worker, the doctor, the psychologist, the contractor, the Minister. You wouldn't have the mansion or the expensive car or the expensive clothing. You wouldn't attract the same friends or associates. You wouldn't attract the same fame and notoriety. So — who would you be?

A lot of people would answer by saying they would be nobody. This is because through conditioning, their understanding of what is truly valuable has been distorted beyond recognition. But consider this: what about the quiet, honest, self-possessed individual you encounter every day when you are alone — when none of the external illusions of value are present to influence you? For a woman, no makeup is required. She could wear rollers and a face mask. She doesn't have to worry whether her shoes match her outfit or watch how she eats. For a man, there is no posturing, no performance of strength for an audience that isn't there. He can listen to love songs or feel what he genuinely feels without fear of being labeled. In those private moments, stripped of every title and every possession, the person who remains — that is who you are. That is the one worth knowing.

A person of genuine character does not have to pretend in order to be accepted — because their acceptance of themselves is not contingent on anyone else's approval. Such an individual is truly honest with himself about his weaknesses, and he works continuously to correct them — not to satisfy others, but because the pursuit of his own integrity demands it. He will not lie to himself when he knows that he is wrong. She will not exaggerate the truth, but will tell it plainly regardless of the benefits or repercussions. She is courteous, and therefore will never sacrifice another person for her own gain or comfort. She will not speak with a forked tongue

— gossiping, diminishing, or destroying another person's reputation to better position herself in the eyes of an audience.

A man or woman of character does the work on themselves so that they become capable of contributing to the development of others. Their movement through the world is deliberate. Their speech carries weight precisely because it is measured. They are fair dealing, and will never take that which is not rightfully theirs. They will never seek to gain at another's expense. They will admit their wrong in the name of peace and progress — not because humility is weakness, but because they understand that clinging to a position you know to be wrong is the weakest thing a person can do. They will never allow pride or personality to cloud a situation, because they have long since understood that pride is not strength — it is a shield built by the insecure to hide what they cannot face.

A man or woman of character never needs to perform. They never need to compete for significance. They never need to diminish another to feel elevated. They are not threatened by the excellence of others, because their sense of value does not come from comparison. It comes from within — from the steady, quiet knowledge of who they are when no one is watching, when there is nothing to gain, when the performance is over and the room is empty and the only voice left is the one that has always known the truth.

This is what character looks like. Not the title. Not the possession. Not the reputation. The person who remains when all of that is gone — steady, honest, self-possessed, and free.

The Key to Character

And so the question with which this chapter began — who am I — is perhaps the only question that has ever mattered. Every chapter in this book has been a different angle of approach to the same answer. The conditioning told you who to be. Fear reinforced it. Selfishness protected it. Irresponsibility extended it. And a lack of discipline kept you returning to it, year after year, wondering why nothing changed.

But underneath all of that — underneath every label that was placed on you and every standard you were handed and every performance you gave in the desperate hope that it would finally be enough — there is a person who has always known exactly who they are. They have been waiting, patiently, through every chapter of the life you have been living for someone else.

The only question now is whether you are ready to meet them.

With all that has been said — are you a man or woman of character?

About the Author

Khalid El Bey

About the Author

Khalid El Bey is an author, public speaker, former elected official, and small business owner whose work spans nearly three decades of community engagement, independent scholarship, and initiatic study.

His formal academic background includes Social Work at Virginia State University in Petersburg, Virginia, and Business, Management, and Economics at Empire State College in Saratoga Springs, New York. He holds a Certificate in Executive Management from the Yale School of Management. To this foundation he has added extensive independent research in history, law, Astrology, Numerology, Qabala, esoteric psychology, and Egyptian and Taoist alchemy — disciplines he approaches not as curiosities but as working tools for understanding the human condition.

He is the founder of the Creative Research Society, an organization whose primary focus is the re-education and empowerment of the so-called African American. He holds senior standing within the Ancient and Primitive Rite of Memphis and

Misraim, one of the oldest and most comprehensive initiatic traditions in the world — a lineage whose roots reach directly into the Egyptian mysteries from which much of Western esoteric knowledge descends.

Mr. Bey has lectured extensively across college and university campuses, community forums, and public platforms along the East Coast and into the Midwest, addressing the origins of human identity, the mechanics of personal development, and the relationship between suppressed history and present circumstance. His written work now spans ten books, each one a different angle of approach to the same essential question: what does a human being have to do to reclaim the life that conditioning took from them?

A former City Councilor in Syracuse, New York, Mr. Bey remains deeply engaged in the political landscape of his community and beyond — bringing the same unsentimental clarity to public life that runs through every page of his writing. He does not separate the personal from the political, the esoteric from the practical, or the historical from the immediate — because in his understanding, they were never separate to begin with.

His guiding principle has not changed: *"In order to change the world, all one has to do is change his mind."*

www.ingramcontent.com/pod-product-compliance
Lightning Source LLC
Chambersburg PA
CBHW070857050426
42453CB00012B/2247